Let's Discuss

ENERGY RESOURCES

Water, Wave, and Tidal Power

Richard and Louise Spilsbury

PowerKiDS press.
New York

Published in 2012 by
The Rosen Publishing Group Inc.
29 East 21st Street,
New York, NY 10010

First Edition

Editorial Director: Rasha Elsaeed
Produced for Wayland by Discovery Books Ltd
Managing Editor: Rachel Tisdale
Designer: Ian Winton
Illustrator: Stefan Chabluk
Picture Researcher: Tom Humphrey

Library of Congress Cataloging-in-Publication Data

Spilsbury, Richard, 1963-
Water, wave, and tidal power / by Richard Spilsbury and Louise Spilsbury. – 1st ed.
p. cm – (Let's discuss energy resources)
Includes index.
ISBN 978-1-4488-5263-5 (lib. bdg.)
1. Water-power–Juvenile literature. 2. Hydraulic engineering–Juvenile literature.
I. Spilsbury, Louise. II. Title. III. Series.

TC146.S65 2012
333.91'4–dc22

2010046937

Photographs:
Corbis: p. 13 (Tugela Ridley/EPA); Dr. I J Stevenson: p. 29; FLPA: p. 10 (Martin B Withers); Getty Images: p. 8 (Chris Niedenthal/Time Life), p. 24 (STRDEL/AFP); Marine Current Turbines Ltd.: p. 17; NS Power: p. 16 & title page; Pelamis: p. 18, p. 25; Practical Action: p. 14 (Zul), p. 15 (Ana Castañeda); Rentricity Inc.: p. 26; Shutterstock: cover (Colin Stitt), p. 4 (J Helgason), p. 6 & imprint page (Lee Prince), p. 11 (Kirk Geisler), p. 21 (Harris Shiffman), p. 22 (Iurii Konoval), p. 28 & cover background (Mana Photo); Voith Hydro Wavegen Limited: p. 19; Wikimedia: p. 5 (Herr Stahlhoefer), p. 12 (Miniwiki).

Manufactured in China
CPSIA Compliance Information: Batch #WAS1102PK: For Further Information contact Rosen Publishing, New York, New York at 1-800-237-9932

Contents

The words in **bold** can be found in the glossary on page 31.

Water Power as an Energy Resource

Water is an energy resource that people have used for centuries to help them to do their work. In the past, the power of moving water turned giant wheels that ground wheat or made machines work. Today, most water power is used to generate electricity.

Growing Demand

Today we are using far more electrical machines and electricity than in the past. Most electricity is generated by burning **fossil fuels**, such as coal and gas. A third fossil fuel, oil, is used mostly as fuel in vehicles. Fossil fuels formed millions of years ago from ancient living things, so there is a limited amount on Earth. They are known as **nonrenewable** energy resources because no more fossil fuels are forming as they are used up.

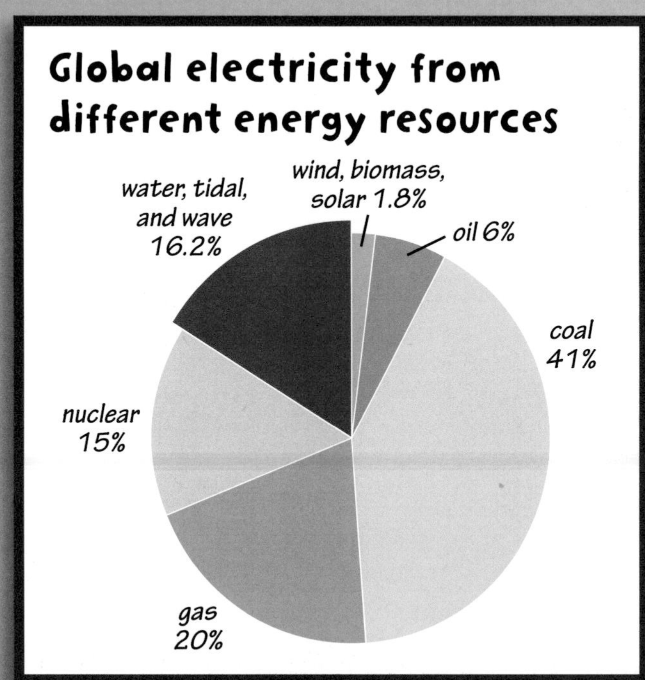

Fossil Fuel Problems

When we burn fossil fuels in vehicles or in power plants to release their energy, we also release gases into the **atmosphere**. Some of these gases including nitrous oxides cause air **pollution** that can harm the environment and damage people's health. Carbon dioxide produced by burning fossil fuels is a **greenhouse gas**. It builds up in the Earth's atmosphere and traps heat from the Sun. As more greenhouse gases build up, more heat is trapped. Most scientists think this is causing **global warming**.

Fossil fuel power supplies around two-thirds of all electricity, but over 90 percent of global energy demand for transportation, electricity, and heating combined.

Global Warming and Climate

The Earth's **climate** has changed naturally throughout history. For example, Antarctica was once covered in forest, but is now much colder and is covered by ice. However, since people started to use lots of fossil fuels over 200 years ago, global warming seems to be changing climates very rapidly. Many places are much hotter, dryer, or wetter than they once were, and these changes are causing extreme weather problems such as floods and droughts.

Power companies around the world control and use the flow of water to generate electricity.

Why discuss water power?

Alternatives to fossil fuel power are renewable energy resources, such as sunlight, wind, and moving water. Water power supplies nearly one-fifth of the world's electricity. Most of this is hydroelectric power made using fresh water moving in rivers or from reservoirs. Tidal power uses the movement of ocean tides, while wave power uses the movement of ocean waves to generate electricity. This book looks at the advantages and disadvantages of water power today and how it can help meet our future energy demands.

Hydroelectric Power

A motorboat has an engine that spins a propeller. This pushes against the water to move the boat forward. Hydroelectric power works a little like this in reverse! Moving water pushes against a turbine and makes it spin like a propeller. This spinning motion is used to produce electricity.

Moving Water

Water in a river has movement energy, or **kinetic energy**. The water moves because of the force of **gravity** pulling the water downhill toward the oceans. The drop in height of the river along its length is called the **head of water**. The head of water increases as the slope gets steeper. The amount of kinetic energy depends on the head of water, but also how much water is moving. There is more force in a wide, deep river than a shallow, narrow river moving down the same slope.

Rivers and Reservoirs

Power companies sometimes use moving river water for hydroelectric power, but mostly get the moving water from reservoirs. Reservoirs are deep, wide man-made lakes that trap river water. The large volume and weight of water in a reservoir has stored or **potential energy**. When water is released from a reservoir down narrow tubes, this potential energy changes into powerful kinetic energy.

The biggest waterfalls in the world have enormous kinetic energy. In some, enough water to fill 15 Olympic swimming pools flows past each minute.

Turbine to Electricity

A turbine has angled blades that convert the strong push of water into a spinning movement. For the blades to spin at their maximum speed, water is usually directed onto them using tubes and sometimes jets. The turbine converts kinetic into mechanical energy in a shaft that spins a generator. This machine generates electricity by rotating coils of wire within a circle of magnets.

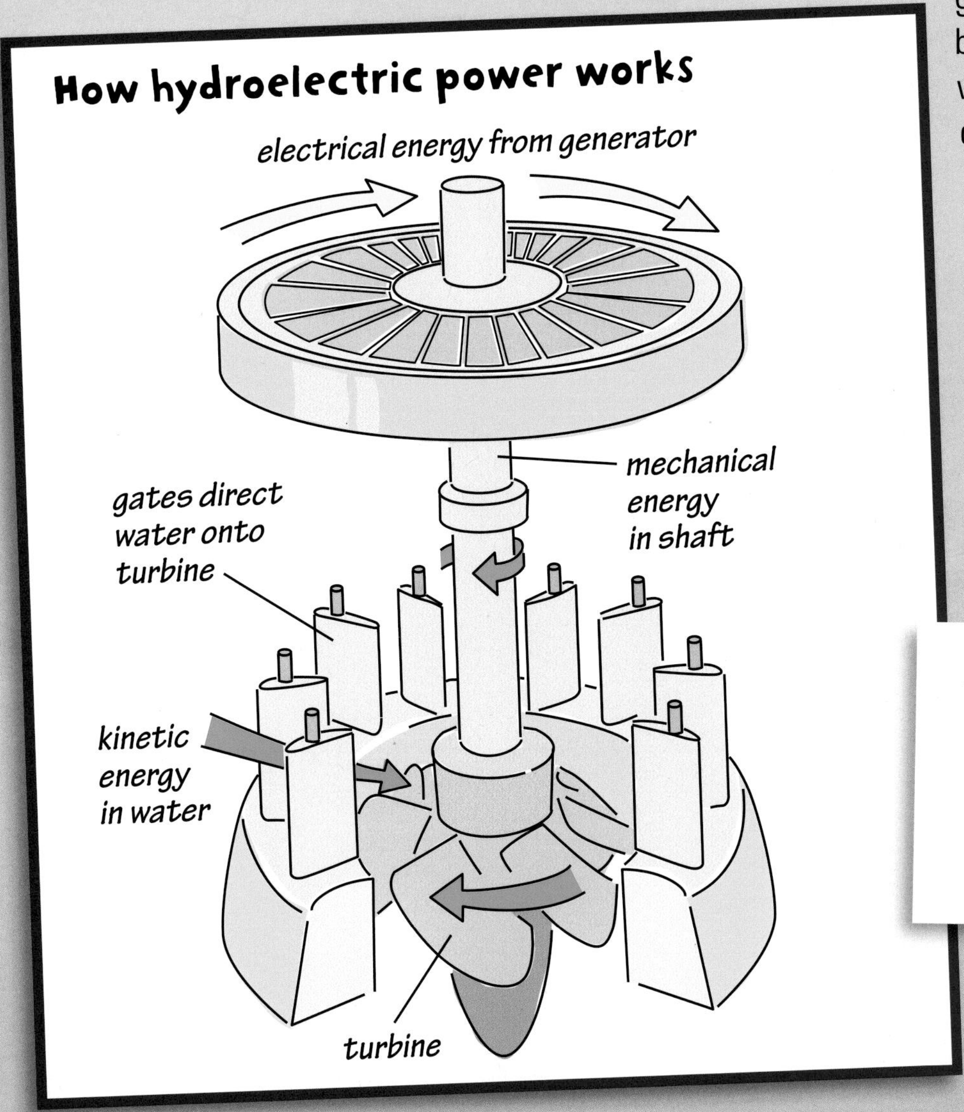

How hydroelectric power works

electrical energy from generator

mechanical energy in shaft

gates direct water onto turbine

kinetic energy in water

turbine

This simple diagram shows how kinetic energy in water changes into electrical energy using a turbine and generator.

Energy and Power

Energy is the ability to do work. A toaster gets energy to toast bread from electricity. Energy can be measured in units called joules. Power is the rate at which energy is used or sent, although sometimes the word is used to describe electrical energy. A laptop computer needs 45 watts, or joules per second, of power to make it work. Big hydroelectric generators make lots of power that we measure in bigger units. A kilowatt (kW) is 1,000 watts and a megawatt (MW) is 1 million watts.

Hydroelectric Dams

Most hydroelectric reservoirs are made by building strong walls called dams across rivers. These trap the water in natural valleys. The turbines and generators are built into the dam structure to form water power plants.

Building a Dam

Engineers design hydroelectric dam walls to be strongest and thickest at the base. This is because the pressure or push of water is greatest at the bottom due to the weight of water above. The wall of the Hoover Dam on the Colorado River is 656 feet (200 meters) thick at the base. It contains enough concrete to fill 660 Olympic-sized swimming pools! When dams are built, other types of **infrastructure** have to be built, too, such as a network of cables and pylons to take the electricity away, and roads for workers to access the power station.

The generators in big hydroelectric dams are as wide as a bus and generate up to 700 MW.

Dam Locations

The best locations for hydroelectric dams are between the rocky banks of powerful rivers that can refill reservoirs as water is used. Many of the major world rivers, such as the Mekong in Vietnam and the Nile in Egypt, have hydroelectric dams. China generates more hydroelectric power than any other country, mostly from the enormous Three Gorges Dam on the Yangtze River. However, countries with smaller rivers still build hydroelectric dams, they just need more of them. Norway has 850 hydroelectric dams that together make nearly all of the country's electricity.

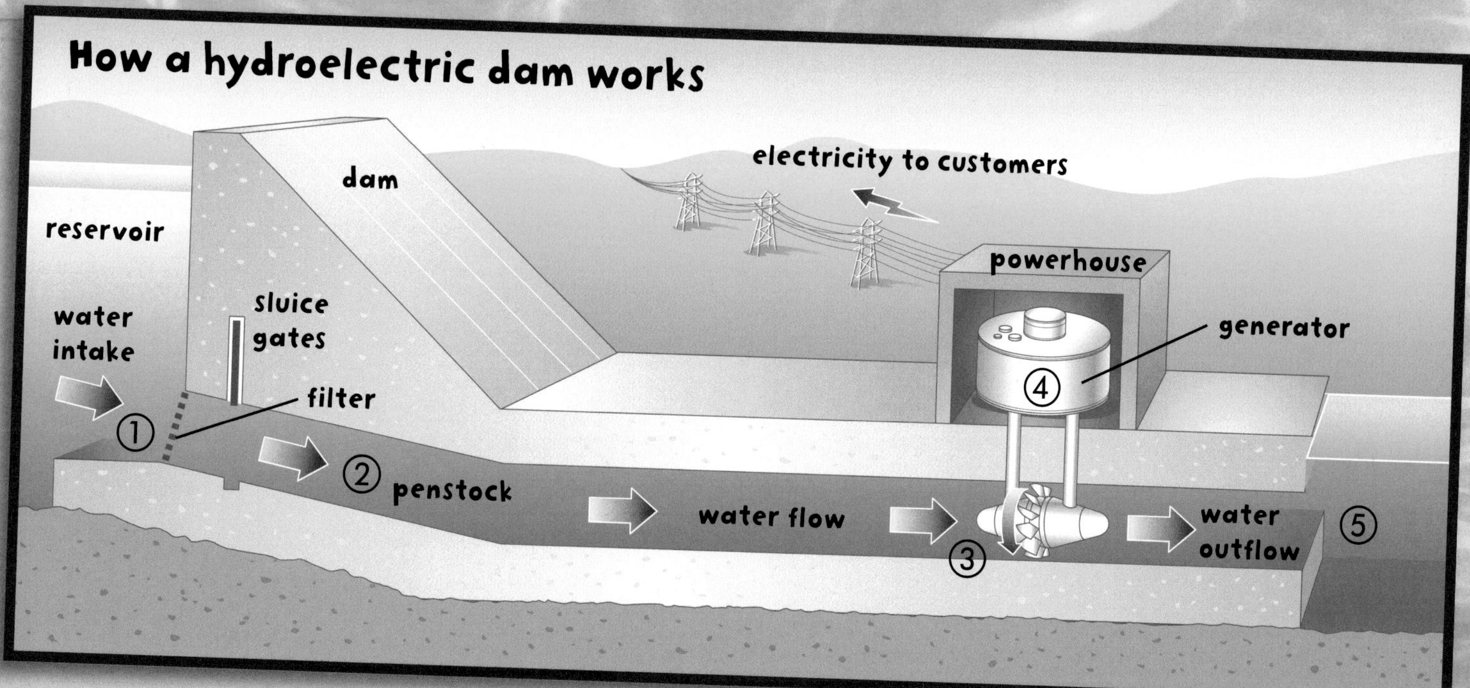

Inside a Dam

1 Water moves from the reservoir through a filter to remove debris that could damage the turbine. **Sluice gates** are opened or closed to control how much water flows. For example, more water is released by day when more electricity is used than at night.

2 The water rushes down an angled tunnel called a **penstock**.

3 Deep within the dam is a chamber with turbines. The biggest turbines are wider than the length of a bus.

4 A generator spins above each turbine and the electricity generated is carried away through power lines.

5 Water that has passed through the turbine has lost much of its kinetic energy. It is usually carried away in the river.

Using Two Reservoirs

A few hydroelectric power plants, including Dinorwig, North Wales, UK, have two reservoirs and are not fed water by a river. They are used for generation when there is higher demand for electricity than other power stations can produce, such as at certain times of day. Then water moves from the top reservoir past the turbines, and collects in the lower reservoir. At night, when other power stations are making more electricity than needed, Dinorwig uses some electricity to pump the water back up the mountain.

Hydroelectricity and the Environment

Hydroelectric dams block rivers to trap water in valleys in order to form reservoirs. Dam-building has many different impacts on rivers, land, and the atmosphere.

How Dams Change Environments

The water level in a reservoir is much higher than the original river level. It floods areas of farmland, woodland, and other environments. This washes lots of soil and rock into the water to add to the sediment normally carried by the river. The build up of sediment can clog up the reservoir.

Power companies release reservoir water through dams when they need to make electricity. They may build up water for long periods to make sure there is a good head of water. This means that water does not always flow, or flows in smaller amounts **downstream**, or below, a dam. Lakes and wetlands downstream get less water and may dry up. This is made worse if people remove reservoir water for other reasons, such as the **irrigation** of farmland or for drinking water.

Dead trees are all that remains of a forest by the Zambezi River, in East Africa, which was flooded to create Lake Kariba reservoir, behind the Kariba hydroelectric dam.

Wildlife is affected by these changes. Animals such as moose feed, shelter, and rest in shallow water, and eat river-edge plants. When forests are flooded for reservoirs, these animals may find it difficult to survive. Dams may block the movement of river animals such as fish. For instance, one reason Yangtze sturgeon are highly endangered is that the Three Gorges Dam blocks the fish's route to breeding places.

Let's Discuss

Is hydroelectric power better for the atmosphere than fossil fuels?

Yes:

No Fuel
Hydroelectric dams burn no fuel. For example, generating electricity with the Three Gorges Dam rather than fossil fuel power plants has prevented millions of tons of carbon dioxide from entering the atmosphere.

Clean Generation
Dams release no polluting gases while generating that can cause environmental problems.

No:

Worse Gases
When valleys are flooded to create hydroelectric reservoirs, the plants underwater rot and release a greenhouse gas called methane. This gas stays in the atmosphere for longer and traps more heat than carbon dioxide.

Deforestation
Hydroelectric power stations are a major cause of deforestation, especially in tropical rain forest areas with big rivers.

On balance, using hydroelectric power is better for the atmosphere than using fossil fuel power.

Impacts of Dams on People

The development of a hydroelectric power plant can bring great benefits to a region. New industries move in to use the electricity, and they bring new jobs and wealth. However, these dams and reservoirs can cause problems for residents, too.

Moving People

The land that has to be flooded to make a reservoir may have villages and farmland on it. Many people are **displaced** or forced to move away in order for dams to be built. In China, the Three Gorges Dam displaced around 2 million people. People downstream from dams may also be forced to move. Slower, emptier rivers are often unsuitable for fishing or for transporting goods. People who work in these industries then have to search for work elsewhere. When people are displaced, they often have no choice where they move. Some people end up in crowded new villages with few job opportunities. There may be further displacement and also injuries and even deaths if dams burst and flood downstream land.

In 2008, an earthquake in southwestern China killed 80,000 people soon after a nearby hydroelectric reservoir was filled. Some scientists think the weight of water caused the earthquake.

Diseases Caused by Reservoirs

Areas of still water such as reservoirs and rivers that have been slowed by dams are ideal places for insects such as mosquitoes to breed. In tropical countries, mosquitoes spread diseases such as malaria that kill millions of people each year. There is also the danger that harmful chemicals can wash from submerged buildings, farmland, and factories. This can make reservoir water poisonous.

Let's Discuss

The effect of Lake Volta on Ghana.

Lake Volta in Ghana is the world's largest hydroelectric reservoir. It was built in the 1960s to provide power for a new aluminum industry. The country had lots of a type of rock containing aluminum but not enough electricity to extract the metal from the rock. Building the reservoir displaced around 80,000 people.

Advantages:

Electricity

Lake Volta gave Ghana large amounts of electricity for the first time. Ghana also sold extra electricity to neighboring countries, such as Benin.

More Work

The lake increased the aluminum, fishing, and tourism industries in Ghana.

These children work in the fishing industry on Lake Volta picking small fish caught in nets.

Disadvantages:

Forced Labor

Many people displaced by the reservoir, including children, are forced to work in the fishing industry because they cannot earn enough from farming on the land they have moved to.

Disease

Farm chemicals that have washed into slow rivers around Lake Volta have made lots of weeds grow. The weeds are home to snails that spread diseases, so the water is not safe to drink or swim in.

On balance, Lake Volta has not benefited most Ghanaians, breaking down their communities and livelihoods.

Hydroelectric Power without Dams

Around the world, small systems of turbines in rivers or other water channels supply the small amounts of electricity needed by individual families, businesses, or communities. This kind of small-scale electricity production is known as microgeneration.

Why Microgeneration?

Communities located in remote areas often use microgeneration where there is no electricity supply. More than 1.5 billion people worldwide do not have **household electricity**, because there is no **grid** (network of cables and pylons) to carry electricity from power stations. Most of these people live in less developed, poor countries.

Some people use microgeneration because they have good resources of fast-moving water to operate hydroelectric turbines. Most hydroelectric microgeneration happens in mountainous regions where there is lots of meltwater from snowy mountain tops in streams and small rivers moving down steep slopes. These places range from Alaska and Tasmania to the Andes and the Himalayas. In Nepal, there are around 2,000 mountain villages that make hydroelectricity by microgeneration.

In this microgeneration installation in Mbuiru village, Kenya, river water is channeled off upstream and moves fast down a penstock into the turbine in the shed.

How Microgeneration Works

The simplest microgeneration system has a turbine with a generator fixed in a steep river or stream. Other types have a pool next to a river or waterfall where there is a good head of water. The pool is connected to a turbine lower down the slope by a long pipe or channel penstock. Turbines used for microgeneration are shaped more like propellers than water wheels because these shapes spin better in smaller amounts of fast-moving water.

Many microgeneration systems are made by local communities using local materials, such as bamboo pipes or recycled metal, in the turbines. Bigger systems that can generate more electricity, for larger communities or businesses, are often constructed using more expensive technology.

Two technicians check the turbine and generator equipment in a small hydroelectric station in Yanacancha, Peru.

CASE STUDY Power Creek, Alaska

Factories in the remote town of Cordova in Alaska prepare and either can or freeze salmon from local rivers so it can be transported for sale elsewhere. The factories need lots of electricity to process the fish, but the town is off the grid and could only get electricity by burning fuel oil. This was so expensive that the salmon industry was struggling. Today, they have a new microgeneration system, with a wide concrete pipe that carries water 1 mile (1.6 km) down a mountain to two large turbines. This newly named "Power Creek" saves the community $1 million each year on fuel.

Tidal Power

Tidal power systems use the energy in seawater to generate electricity. They harness the daily movement of tides toward and away from coastal land, or fast-moving currents in underwater channels.

Trapping and Releasing Seawater

Tidal **barrages** are like wide, low dams built across shallow bays and **estuaries**. These coastal areas are good places for barrages because their shape narrows toward land. They funnel tidal water moving in, so the water level gets higher than it would on a straight area of coast.

Water is flowing from left to right through the Annapolis Royal tidal barrage and past its turbines to generate electricity.

When the tide comes in, the barrage blocks the flow of seawater toward land. The trapped water creates a high head of water on the sea side of the barrage. At high tide, or when the sea level is highest, sluice gates in the barrage are opened. The water that is released flows past turbines inside the barrage. These turn generators that make electricity.

When the tide starts to go out, the sluice gates are closed. This time, the barrage traps water on the land side to create a head of water there. At low tide, this water is released to generate electricity. Tidal lagoons work just like tidal barrages by trapping and releasing water. However, they are circular walls built in estuaries rather than across them.

The Bay of Fundy

The Bay of Fundy, Canada, has the world's highest tides of up to 56 feet (17 meters). Every day, more seawater flows in and out of the bay than flows through all the rivers in the world! Annapolis Royal tidal power plant was built in 1984 to generate electricity using the tides. It makes enough electricity for around 4,000 Canadian homes each year.

Underwater Turbines

Some tidal power is made using underwater turbines that capture the energy in moving tidal currents. The currents turn the turbine blades in the same way as water from a hydroelectric reservoir. Power companies usually install several turbines that they attach individually to the seafloor or build into underwater walls that they call reefs.

Tidal Locations

Power companies build tidal barrages where there are very high tides, because then there are big heads of water with which to generate electricity. They install underwater turbines where currents are very fast and can turn the turbines quickly. Current speed depends on the shape of the sea floor, for example, currents flow fast in the gap between two islands. Tidal power plants are expensive to build, so in 2009, there were still only six tidal power plants in operation in the world. These are in North America, Russia, South Korea, France, and Northern Ireland.

Wide underwater turbines capture the kinetic energy in underwater currents.

Wave Power

Wind blows against the surface of the sea and creates waves that are packed with kinetic energy. However, power companies have only recently started to convert wave energy into electricity. The first wave power station or farm only started operating in 2008, but more wave farms are planned in places where waves are strongest.

At Sea

There are different types of technology to capture wave energy out at sea. One technology uses **buoys** that rise and fall as waves pass by. Machines inside the buoys convert the movement into electricity. This is carried from the buoy through cables on the sea floor to land.

The most common wave power technology is Pelamis. Pelamis consists of a row of four or five long floating cylinders hinged together. Each cylinder is the size of a train car. The whole unit is attached to the ocean floor with strong cables. When one cylinder rises higher than another, the movement pushes a small amount of oil through narrow tubes inside Pelamis. The force of the oil spins turbines and these spin generators to produce electricity. Power companies can install several Pelamis machines together in a wave power farm to generate more electricity.

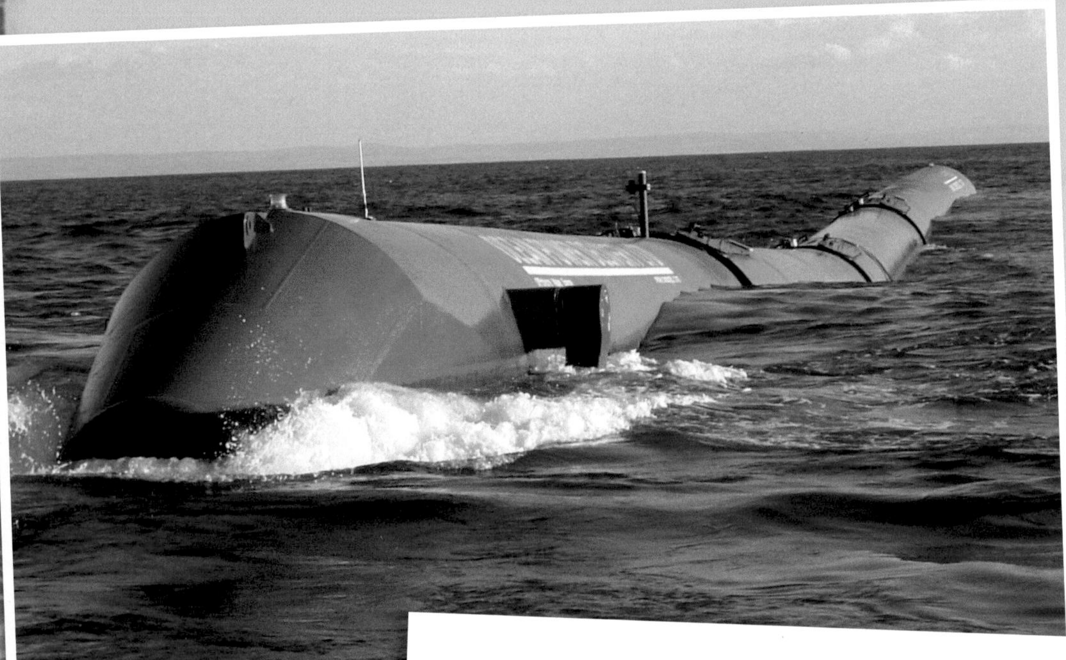

As waves move along the length of Pelamis, the cylinders rise and fall in sequence. Electricity is generated where the cylinders hinge together.

On Coasts

Other wave power technology is built into coasts where powerful waves hit land. Limpet is the name of a concrete chamber built onto rocks. The air inside is pushed out and through a turbine when waves enter the chamber. Then when seawater drains out, air is sucked from outside the chamber into and through the turbine. Therefore, both the rise and fall of waves is used to generate electricity.

Limpet converts the crash of waves against rocky shores into electricity.

The Best Waves

Some places on Earth have much stronger waves than others. Winds form when the Sun warms some of the air above the Earth's surface. The warm air rises and other, cooler air moves in to take its place. Some of the strongest winds blow in regions such as northern Canada, northern Europe, and southern Africa. Here cold, polar air blows toward warm air over land, especially during the winter. Waves build up speed over large oceans, such as the Atlantic, because there are few obstacles to get in the way of the wind. Waves also get higher closer to coasts, because the seawater piles up as the sea floor gets shallower.

Problems with Tidal and Wave Power

Tidal and wave power are useful renewable energy sources, but they do have some problems. Tidal power can have major impacts on coastal waters and neither tidal nor wave power can generate electricity all of the time.

Variations in Tidal Power

Tides rise and fall each day because the Moon pulls on the oceans. Tidal barrages can only generate electricity at low or high tide when there is a head of water built up on one side of the barrage. Then the water can spin the turbines fast enough for about 1–3 hours before the levels on either side are too similar. The height of high and low tides also changes as the Earth moves around the Sun through the year. This means the amount of electricity generated rises and falls, too. Even so, the biggest tidal barrages can generate lots of electricity. For example, the planned Severn **estuary** barrage, in the UK, could generate as much electricity as 12 nuclear power plants.

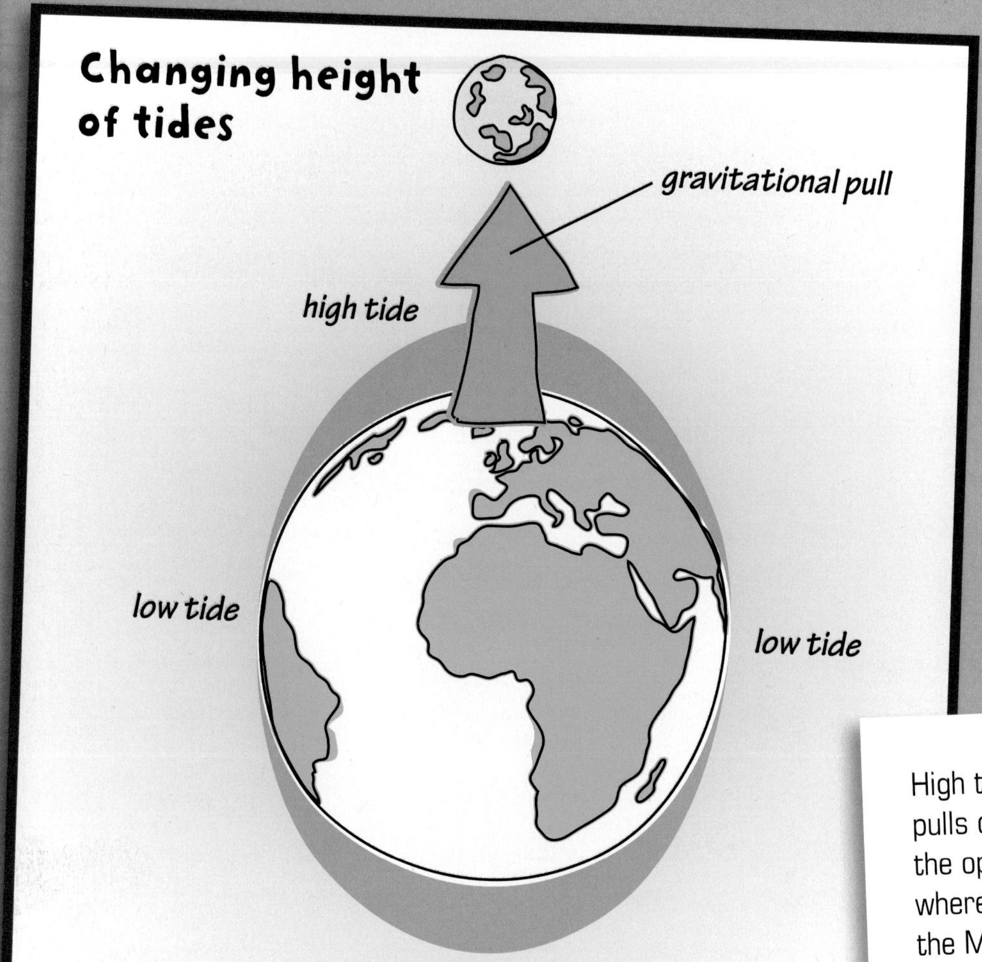

Changing height of tides

High tides form as the Moon pulls on the oceans and also on the opposite side of the planet, where the Earth is pulled toward the Moon more than the water there. The pull of the Moon is called gravitational pull.

Barrage Impacts

Tidal power barrages obstruct the movements of large amounts of seawater. The large area of trapped water can encourage some animals, such as fish, to breed in estuaries, but estuary birds cannot find the worms and other small animals they eat from the mud. Another issue is that sewage or chemicals washed off coastal farmland into estuaries by rain can build up in estuary water behind barrages. This pollution can harm estuary organisms.

Avocets need coastal mud to find the food they need to survive.

Let's Discuss

Wave power is more reliable than tidal power.

For:

Waves Everywhere
There are only about 40 places worldwide with enough tidal variation for power companies to build large tidal power plants.

More Power
Using current technology, wave power could supply as much electricity as is used globally today, but tidal power can only supply a fraction of this.

Against:

Through the Year
Tides rise and fall twice a day every day, all year round, but waves are more variable in power through the year.

Damaging Waves
The force of waves can easily damage or detach wave power machines. Strong wave technology is often very expensive.

Wave power is a bigger energy resource overall than tidal power, but it varies more and may be more expensive to harness.

Demand and Supply of Water Power

The amount of electricity people need in different parts of the world and the amount that hydroelectric power stations can supply varies for many reasons.

A hydroelectric dam in Ukraine at night. In many places, rivers keep flowing day and night all year round so dams keep generating.

Electricity Demand

The amount of electricity individuals and businesses use or consume varies. For example, in places such as Canada or New Zealand, there is greater demand for electricity for heating during cold winters than during warmer summers. People in more developed countries, who often use many electrical machines from dishwashers to computers, consume more electricity overall than people in less developed countries. For example, in 2005, an average person in Canada used 17 MWh, which is ten times more than an average person in Costa Rica.

Power Price

Hydroelectric stations can supply electricity all year round in places where rivers flow constantly. The cost for a kWh of hydroelectricity is similar to that from fossil fuel power plants that burn coal or gas. It is cheaper than electricity from any other renewable energy resource, including tidal and wave power. Tidal power and wave power are expensive and at present cannot meet demand for more than a few thousand people, because there are few operating power stations.

"If you can connect the grid to hydro power, you've got that as a backup battery."

Arnulf Jaeger-Walden, European Commission's Institute for Energy

Supply Problems

In some places hydroelectricity cannot meet demand, even if there are many hydroelectric stations. For example, in very hot places, such as Kenya, rivers may dry up and in very cold places, such as Canada, rivers may freeze over. Then power companies must generate electricity using other energy resources to meet demand.

CASE STUDY Power Sharing

The Nordic countries of Sweden, Norway, Denmark, and Finland sell electricity to each other so they always have enough. Around 99 percent of electricity from Norway is generated from hydroelectric dams. In the winter, Norwegians use more electricity, for example, for heating, than the dams can provide, so power companies buy electricity from Finland, Sweden, and Denmark to meet demand. In the summer, when rivers are at their fullest, Norway makes more hydroelectricity than it can use, and sells some to the other countries. For example, Denmark buys hydroelectricity to make up for there being less wind in summer to operate its wind turbines.

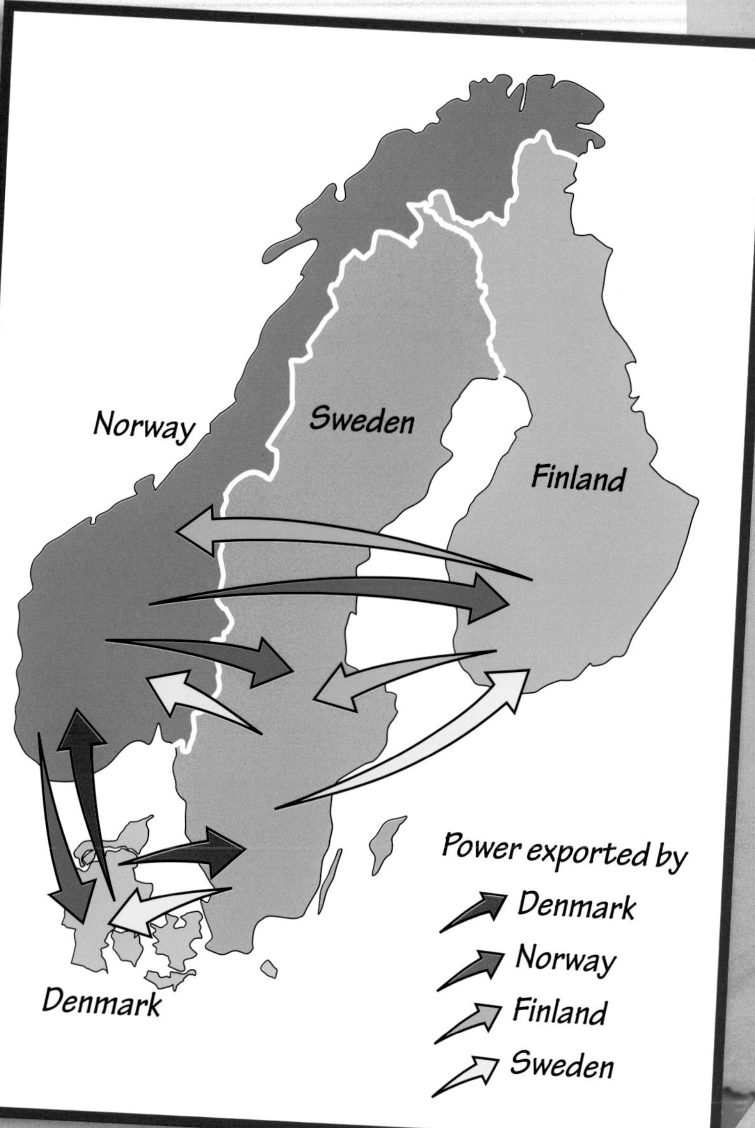

This diagram shows the trade in electricity between Nordic countries. The longer the arrow, the more electricity traded.

How Governments Affect Water Power

Many countries around the world have agreed targets to cut the amount of greenhouse gases they produce. The problem is that they still need to supply enough electricity for their people and industries. One way to meet targets is to increase the amount of renewable energy, because this produces little or no greenhouse gases.

Paying for Power

One way governments encourage renewable power is to pay more for renewable electricity. Paying extra to make something cheaper so more people buy it is called **subsidizing**. For example, in 2005, the Portuguese government agreed to pay 0.25€ ($0.30) more for each kWh of electricity from the Pelamis wave farm than it will pay for fossil fuel electricity. This subsidy does not sound like much, but it means that wave power is closer in price to fossil fuel power. If companies can charge more for hydroelectric, tidal, and wave power, then more power companies will invest in setting up more water power installations.

When Water Power Causes Conflict

Many rivers run through several countries. The rivers are shared resources not only for hydroelectric power but also for uses such as irrigation. If one country takes a lot of water from a shared river, it can cause disagreements. For example, in India, the government built the Baghilar hydroelectric dam across a river that runs into the Indus River in Pakistan. In some parts of Pakistan, the Indus is drying up. In 2009, Pakistani terrorists threatened to destroy the Baghilar dam to protect their water supply.

Building a dam, as here in India, is a massive, complex, and expensive engineering project.

Let's Discuss

Should governments subsidize water power?

Yes:

Be Fair
In a way, fossil fuel power is already massively subsidized because power companies do not have to pay for the effects of global warming caused by the greenhouse gases they produce.

Better Option
All power technologies have their environmental problems, but it is better to subsidize a renewable than a nonrenewable energy resource.

The Portuguese government hopes its Pelamis wave farm can meet the electricity demand of around 15,000 Portuguese households and prevent more than 65,000 tons of carbon dioxide getting into the atmosphere.

No:

Unproven Technology
Wave power technology is unproven for generating electricity over long periods. For example, in 2009, several Pelamis machines stopped generating because seawater got inside them.

Small Amounts
Wave and tidal power only generate small amounts of electricity. It would take 10,000 Pelamis machines to generate as much as one nuclear power plant.

Subsidizing water power is very important for encouraging power companies to reduce greenhouse gases. However, often governments have found it best to use different ways to generate the electricity their countries need.

New Water Power Technology

From the nineteenth century up to the 1960s, the only water power technology available was hydroelectric in rivers. Then tidal and wave power technologies became available, too. Future new technologies could make water power much more widely used than today.

Personal Water Power

Imagine if flushing the toilet turned the light on! Water moves fast out of toilets and through water pipes. Rentricity is a company developing small turbines and generators that fit into water pipes and can produce electricity from this energy source. Another company in China has designed shoes that generate electricity as you walk. The sole of each shoe contains a narrow bladder of water with a mini turbine inside connected to a tiny generator. As we walk, we put our weight first on the heel and then the ball of the foot. This movement squeezes water in the bladder past the turbine. Wires from the generator can take the electricity to devices the walker may want to use, such as an MP3 player!

Rentricity workers installing a turbine into the downhill water pipes under the streets in Rhode Island to generate electricity from high-pressure household water.

Ocean Heat to Electricity

Ocean thermal energy power is a method of using the temperature difference between cold, deep seawater and warmer surface seawater to make electricity. In the simplest system, warm seawater is used to evaporate liquid called ammonia into a gas. The gas moves a turbine and generator. Cold seawater is used to condense the ammonia gas back into liquid so it can be used again. Another system evaporates the warm seawater to make steam to turn turbines. The cold seawater then condenses the water vapor into fresh water that can be used to help grow crops and for drinking!

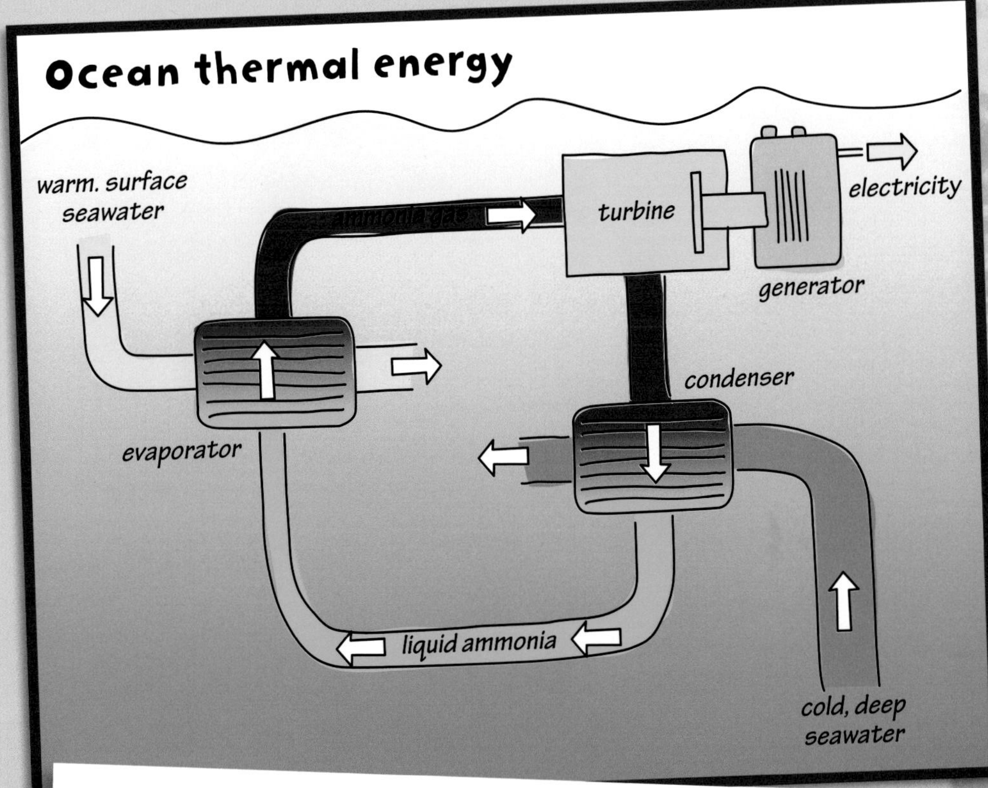

Ocean thermal energy uses the temperature difference between surface and deep seawater to generate electricity.

CASE STUDY Copying Fish

The water in canals, waterways, and many rivers often moves too slowly for normal turbines to spin fast enough to run a generator. Researchers at the University of Michigan studying the way river fish use the power of swirling water found near cylindrical shapes in slow-moving water to give them a push. The researchers developed technology that can generate power in a similar way. The swirling movements force cylinders on springs up and down. This movement is then converted into electricity. The researchers estimate that each cubic yard of slow-moving water could produce about 50 watts of power.

The Future for Water Power

Water power is renewable, uses no fuel, and produces less greenhouse gas than nonrenewable energy resources. However, at present, the majority of water power comes from hydroelectric dams that still cause environmental and human problems. So, how will water power develop in the future?

Hydroelectric Power in the Future

Hydroelectric power has the potential to supply half of the world's electricity needs, for example, if existing dams were converted into hydroelectric dams. However, most new hydroelectric power will be in the form of microgeneration. This is because more countries and power companies will avoid building big hydroelectric dam and reservoir projects due to their environmental problems.

Wave and Tidal Power in the Future

The world's population uses about 20 trillion kWh of electricity each year at present, which takes the equivalent of 4 million big coal power plants to produce. Scientists think demand could rise to 30 trillion kWh by 2030. Around 70 percent of the Earth is moving ocean water, and this vast resource could be used to generate more electricity than we use today.

"Tidal stream energy is no longer a nice-to-have. It is a must-have."

Martin Wright, Marine Current Turbines, 2009

Waves will grow in importance as a future energy resource for coastal countries.

Growth Areas

The main increase in wave and tidal power will come in places where there are powerful waves and high tides, such as off northwestern Europe and North America, southern Australasia, South America, and Africa. The hope is that the technology to harness water power will also get cheaper if it is used more widely. Another reason the price of wave and tidal power could get closer to fossil fuel power is that future governments might make power companies pay for the environmental impacts caused by their fossil fuel power stations.

Coastal countries around the world are considering tidal current turbines as part of their energy mix.

CASE STUDY

A Tidal Future in South Korea?

Tidal power is expanding rapidly in South Korea because of its high tides and the strong tidal currents off its coasts. By 2015, the country could have the world's largest tidal power plant. It will have 300 tidal turbines each measuring 65 feet (20 meters). They will be set up at the bottom of a deep channel off the coast where tidal currents are fastest. Each turbine will be mounted on a 2,750-ton (2,500-tonne) frame that contains the generator. The installation should generate 300 MW of renewable electricity, which is enough to power 200,000 South Korean homes. However, the future of these coastal power stations depends partly on global warming. Extreme winds and storms called typhoons are forming more regularly over the South China Sea off South Korea. These could easily damage power installations and their infrastructure.

Water Activity

Demonstrate Water Power

In hydroelectric dams, the pipes taking water to the turbines is near the bottom of the reservoir because water flows at higher pressure here and can spin the turbines faster. Here's a simple way to demonstrate this water pressure.

What you need:

- Tall milk or fruit juice carton, empty and clean
- Scissors
- A skewer or wide nail
- Masking tape
- Marker pen
- Ruler

1 Cut the top off the carton with scissors. Carefully make four holes in a vertical row down one side using the skewer. They should be 2.5, 3.5, 5, and 6 inches (6, 9, 12, and 15 cm) from the base.

2 Tape over each hole and then fill the carton to near the top with water.

3 Stand the carton with the holes pointing toward a sink. Untape the bottom hole and measure how far the water shoots out. How does the distance change as more water leaves the carton?

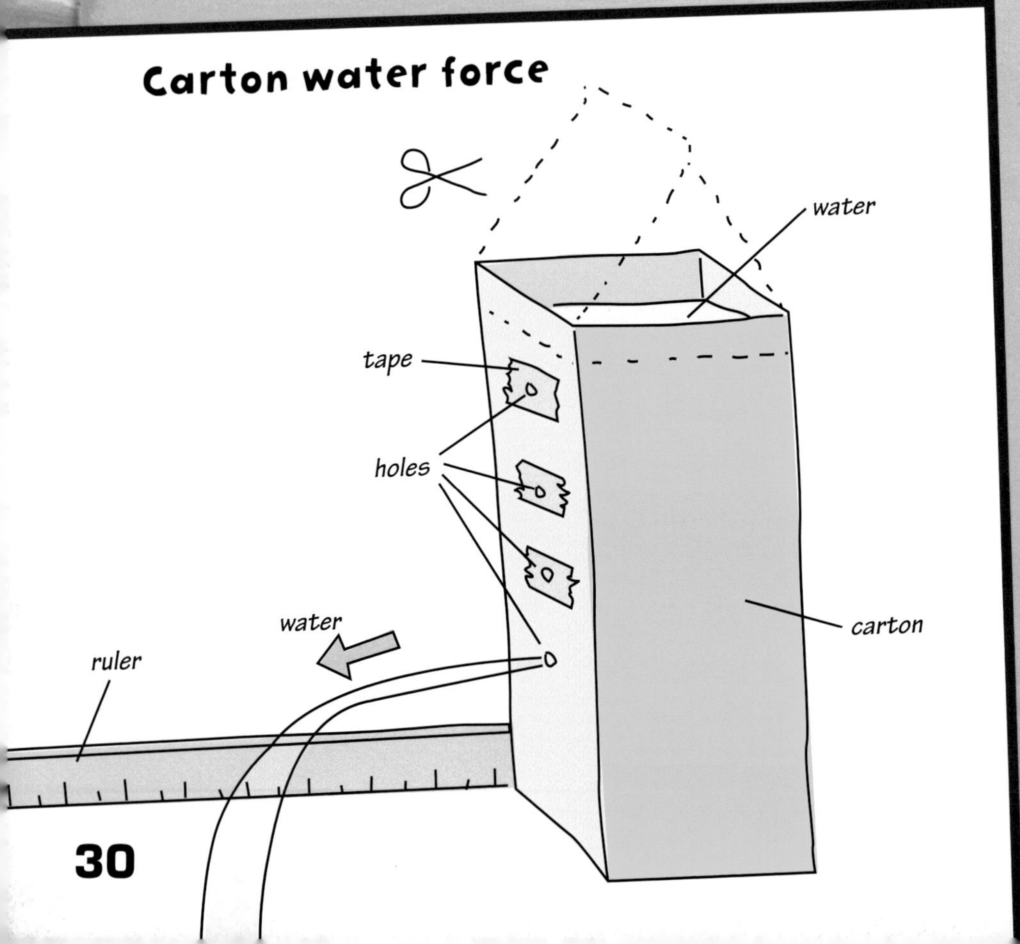

4 Tape up the bottom hole, refill the carton, and then repeat Step 3 but untape each of the other holes one by one. Record your measurements each time. What effect does water depth have on the distances the water shoots out?

Carton water force

Water Topics and Glossary

History

- Find out about the birth of hydroelectricity in the nineteenth century in the U.S. through to the first large hydroelectric dams in the 1930s. What was the role of some of these power plants during World War II?

Geography

- What are the positive impacts of big dams for people apart from hydroelectric power?

Design and Technology

- Design your own wave power machine that can use the rise and fall or push of wave energy, and create a poster advertising its advantages over other designs.

English

- Write a letter to a government energy official of a small island persuading them to use wave and tidal power more than other energy resources.

Science

- Water only fills rivers because of the water cycle. Investigate the ways that the water cycle might be affected by global warming.

Glossary

atmosphere mix of gases surrounding the Earth up to the edge of space.

barrage man-made barrier across a water course such as an estuary.

buoy floating device, usually anchored to the sea floor to prevent loss or damage.

climate normal pattern of weather over long periods.

current flow of water or electricity.

displace cause to move usually as a result of conflict or environmental change.

downstream in the same direction as a river or stream current.

estuary wide, lower part of a river where it meets the sea.

fossil fuel fuel such as coal formed over millions of years from remains of living things.

global warming increase in the average temperature of the atmosphere and oceans.

gravity force of attraction between bodies with mass, such as the Moon, Earth, and Sun.

greenhouse gas gas such as carbon dioxide that stores heat in the atmosphere.

grid system of wires and pylons for sending electricity across a wide area.

head of water difference in height of two bodies of water.

household electricity electricity supplied through the grid to users from power plants.

hydroelectric power using moving fresh water in rivers or from reservoirs to generate electricity.

infrastructure cables, roads, power stations and other structures needed to make a system work.

irrigation to supply farmland with water diverted from rivers or reservoirs using ditches, pumps, pipes and sprinklers.

kinetic energy energy produced by movement.

microgeneration small-scale production of electricity to meet the needs of users.

nonrenewable energy resource such as coal that is running out as it is not replaced when used.

penstock angled channel or pipe taking water to a turbine for hydroelectric power.

pollution harmful substances that make air, water, or soil less safe to use or live in.

potential energy energy stored within a system as a result of an object's height or position.

renewable energy resource that is replaced naturally and can be used without running out.

reservoir man-made freshwater lake, usually formed by damming a river.

sluice gates gate to control the flow of water in a channel.

subsidize pay to support something and encourage its success.

tide daily rise and fall of sea level.

Further Information, Web Sites, and Index

Books

Energy for the Future and Global Warming: Water Power
by Andrew Solway
(Gareth Stevens Publishing, 2007)

Future Energy: Wind and Water
by Jim Holloff
(Abdo Publishing Company, 2010)

The World of Energy: Understanding Water Power
by Polly Goodman
(Gareth Stevens Publishing, 2010)

Web Sites

Due to the changing nature of Internet links, PowerKids Press has developed an online list of Web sites related to the subject of this book. This site is updated regularly. Please use this link to access this list:
http://www.powerkidslinks.com/lder/water/

Index